red signature

DATE DUE

DEMCO 38-296

THE NATIONAL POETRY SERIES

The National Poetry Series was established in 1978 to publish five collections of poetry annually through five participating publishers. The manuscripts are selected by five poets of national reputation. Publication is funded by James A. Michener, the Copernicus Society of America, Edward J. Piszek, the Lannan Foundation, and the Tiny Tiger Foundation.

1996 COMPETITION WINNERS

JEANNE MARIE BEAUMONT
Placebo Effects
Chosen by William Matthews
published by W.W. Norton

A. V. CHRISTIE
Nine Skies
Chosen by Sandra McPherson
published by the University of Illinois Press

JEFF CLARK
The Little Door Slides Back
Chosen by Ray DiPalma
published by Sun & Moon Press

BARBARA CULLY
The New Intimacy
Chosen by Carolyn Forché
published by Viking/Penguin Press

MARY LEADER
Red Signature
Chosen by Deborah Digges
published by Graywolf Press

JUDGE'S STATEMENT

"*Red Signature* is extreme in its approach to experience. Its vision is slant, peripheral, and strange, as if the poet raced toward a horizon as she wrote. At the same time, this work is saturated with detail, work possessing a Bishop-like self-inquiry, a fascination for the world's disparity and symmetry. Sometimes, as I read it, I felt as if I were reading an ancient text translated along the way by many anonymous scribes. Other times the poems appeared entirely rooted in the present, enacting for the first time an essential human ritual that praises being alive."

DEBORAH DIGGES

red signature

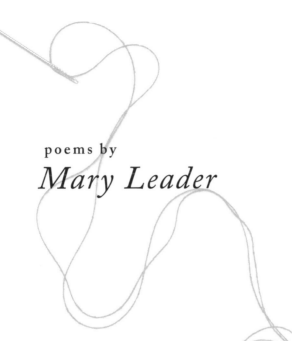

poems by
Mary Leader

GRAYWOLF PRESS

in part by a grant provided
1 an appropriation by
rant from the National
onal support has been
tion, the Lila Wallace-
lation, and other generous
contributions from foundations, corporations, and individuals. To these
organizations and individuals who make our work possible, we offer
heartfelt thanks.

Published by Graywolf Press
2402 University Avenue, Suite 203
Saint Paul, Minnesota 55114

Published in the United States of America

ISBN 1-55597-255-1

2 4 6 8 9 7 5 3 1
First Graywolf Printing, 1997

Library of Congress Catalog Card Number: 96-78741

Cover Painting: Franz Marc, *Grazing Horses IV (The Red Horses)*, 1911,
oil on canvas, 121 × 183 cm. Courtesy of the Busch-Reisinger Museum,
Harvard University Art Museums. Anonymous loan to the Busch-
Reisinger Museum and the Cincinnati Art Museum.

Cover Design: Jeanne Lee

Acknowledgments

Grateful acknowledgment is made to the editors of the following publications in which the poems below, sometimes in different versions, first appeared:

Denver Quarterly: "Linear"

Laurel Moon: "My Son Ted"

Malahat Review: "To a Girl with a Satchel"

Membrane: "Girls' Names"

The Quarterly: "After My Brother Baruch's Bar Mitzvah / Last Night"; "Among Things Held at Arm's Length" (in a different version); "Colter's Elegy"; "Horse Chestnut"; "Middle Daughter's Song"; "Poem"; "Probate"; "Schoolteacher's Ditty" (under the title "Schoolteacher Gets Spring Fever"); and "Trimmed with Eyelet Lace"

Response: A Contemporary Jewish Review: "Oklahoma Passover"; and "The Sign of the Cohens Carved on a Gravestone"

River City: "Girl at Sewing Machine"

Virginia Quarterly Review: "Her Door"

Western Humanities Review: "Photographs (for our children)"

Red Signature

I.

II.

III.

IV.

For Neal Leader

I had begun to sign canvases, but I soon stopped because it seemed too foolish. On one seascape there is a clamorous red signature because I wanted a red note in the green.

VINCENT VAN GOGH

I.

Middle Daughter's Song

I look down on you, Town. I can't prove
That the units you use to bind time are wrong:
    The loaf, the nap, the coin.
When I look up, though, the whole sky scoops!
    Safehold my nine aunts, who are sewing,
My father, storekeeping . . . Sundust on the till.
    Your edge is my hope. I am going.

Probate

3 spools of thread
        1 black
        1 white
        1 blue

2 envelopes
        labeled "Receipts"
        & "Rent Checks—Canceled"

1 pr. steel-rim spectacles, good cond.

2 hypodermic syringes, 1 w/ needle

1 sq. crochet, white cotton

1 skull-bone, some sm. rodent— baby rabbit? mouse?

1 sm. purple bottle— medicine, whiskey, or perfume

2 feathers
        1 mockingbird
        1 blue jay

1 card pearl buttons, $\frac{3}{16}$ inch

Postcard— road disappearing into tree-covered hills
"Greetings from Wister, Okla." 1¢ stamp

Dear Aunt Clara,
  It is very pretty in the   TO:
Mountains but I haven't got   Mrs. Everett R. Hake
Any pictures yet as it has   R.R. #2
Been raining every since we   Shawnee, Oklahoma
Got here.
        Your ~~Neice~~ Niece,
          Edna Rae Wilson

Framed picture of a black-&-white hen, in box w/ note

Dear Aunt Clara,
        Whenever I saw this I just had to get it for you
As it reminded me so much of when I was little. I always
Thought you kept those black and white speckled chickens to
Match the counter in your kitchen.

Well, everbody's fine here in Tulsa. I wish you'd
Let us hear along.
                              Lots of love, Edna

Advertising pad— "Tucker Feed & Seed   Tel. 387"
Black ink, turned purple; some in pencil

I was born & raised in Dawes
County, Nebraska.

My Favorite Flower: the Violet

My Favorite Tree: the White Ash

My Favorite Hymn: When I Come to
        the Cross by the Silent Sea

My husband was Everett R. Hake.
He was first & foremost a farmer.
Which I never did see anything wrong
With. He just wasn't cut out
For them other things.

His main hobby was sketching
And he was awful good at that, least I
Thought he was good at it.
I remember one Sunday afternoon
Not long after we was married
He sat out there on the porch
And sketched my Dad. It was one
Of his best ones, I thought,
Especially around the eyes.
But I recollect Daddy didn't seem
To like it that much. I think that
Sort of hurt Bama's feelings.

In fact I know it did.

When I was a child, my Grandad
Had a matched team of pure white mules.
Named Meeshack & Bendigo
But called them Shack & Ben.
Shack, he had brown eyes

Like a normal mule but Ben, now,
His eyes were pure blue.
Just like a china doll.
Plus he was stone deaf.

I have often noticed this in cats
Too. Whenever you see a cat
Which is pure white with blue eyes,
If you will notice,
Most likely it will be deaf.

I have thought up this—

Three separate times the rooster crowed
    and Peter hung his head.
Before the ghastly day was out
    his Lord was gone for dead.

Three separate times the baby died
    the mother sank with sorrow.
A child who breaches birth today
    will wake with God tomorrow.

By Clara C. Hake

1 magnifying glass, leather case

1 box paper clips

1 ream letterhead

E. R. "Bama" Hake   Rural Route 2
Drilling Contractor   Shawnee, Oklahoma

1 box brads

Letter, white onionskin, no envelope

Dearest Son,
    Here is that recipe you requested I send
Clara—

CHESS PIE
unbaked pie shell
¼ lb. butter
1 ½ C. sugar

¼ t. salt
3 T. flour or corn meal
1 C. cream
1 t. vanilla
2 eggs, beaten
Cream butter & sugar. Add other
ingredients, mixing thoroughly.
Pour into pie shell and bake
at 300° — 45 min. to 1 hr.
Speaking of Clara, I wish you would please
(cont.)
Inform her that I most certainly <u>was</u> sorry about
This baby. I certainly intended <u>no</u> offense. But
Son, she is going to have to buck up, now, that's
All they is to it.
Well you are <u>both</u> welcome in my home at <u>any</u>
Time. I remain, as ever,
Your Loving,
Mother

2 dried-out bottles ink
1 blue
1 black

10–12 empty packs, Lucky Strike cigarettes

2 boxes campaign cards

Everett R. Hake
for
County Commissioner
Pottawatomie Co. Dist. #3
Honest * Hard-Working * Ex-Serviceman

4 pencils, sharpened w/ knife

1 wooden pencil box, full of silver dollars

1 fountain pen, good cond.

After My Brother Baruch's Bar Mitzvah / Last Night

I dreamt I lost my voice, I ran, the loft door
   opened wide.

Below, the chanting hat-stream passed. "Tamara,
    try to hide,"

Ma whispered. David drummed—I twirled, in smoking
     lantern light.

I'd practiced, so I knew my part—my apron
      came untied.

This sky is upside down, white sun, and charcoal
       clouds in flight.

My arm feels cold. I ache. I smell like wet-mowed
        hay inside.

Trimmed with Eyelet Lace

Mother thinks I'm stupid to iron my nightgowns.
She says, "Didn't you ever hear of wash-&-wear?"
She says, "Who's going to see you in your nightgown?"
She says, "Why don't you just sleep in your undies?
Be cheaper." But she can't say much, seeing as how
I buy my own clothes. I work down at the *Democrat*,
Help get the paper out on Wednesday nights,
Plus I grade algebra papers for Mr. Cartmell.
His wife works at the phone company.
I wonder what she is like.
One time when I was in the Style Shoppe, I saw her
Buying a nightgown, one of those nylon kind.
I like cotton a lot better. (It feels nice.)

Doris Ann's Ash Street March

Four old men on
      the one depot bench
Miss Cassie Ellis in
      her black dotted swiss

Her with her hankerchiff
      them in straw hats
Seen the soldier off
      seen him gone

Buy a sack of green beans
      buy-a loaf-a bread
Kids' wagon ticking off
      the sidewalk cracks

How far to Galveston?
      How far to France?
Cad Ellis better
      Come Back!

Colter's Elegy

My prime of youth is but a frost of cares
My feast of joy is but a dish of pain
CHIDIOCK TICHBORNE

I, Michael Wayne Colter, is going to die of starvation.
I will not eat one bite of food in the Pawnee County Jail
From this day forward. March 21, 1980, to March 31, 1980.
I shall leave a will. I would like to be buried beside
My Grandpa, Edgar Merlon Brown.

My Will

I leave my books and bookshelf to my baby cousins Brandon
    and Kyle.
I leave my toys to my cousins also.
I leave my clothes to whoever can fit them.
I leave my clock-radio to my Grandma, Lessie Inez Brown,
    then when she passes on it goes to Lee Ann Willoughby.
I leave my Susan B. Anthony dollars and my $2 bill to
    Lee Ann Willoughby also.
I leave my mom whatever she wants but my step-father
    shall get nothing or he will be cursed.
I leave the rest of my stuff to my mom, Lavonna Gail Colter.

Signed,
Michael Colter

Schoolteacher's Ditty

I wish I were a matchstick drifting
      drifting free on Black Bear Creek

Clouds all stretched out on pallets
      boughs rolling back like a filmstrip
          the wind just waving me on

Noon whistle, go choke on an old chicken bone
      I could not care less

I am just a matchstick drifting
        free and easy on down the creek
            on down to Arkansas

II.

Horse Chestnut

One Time

It was here, here
By this very tree, late
At night in the snow . . .
Your beard
Chilled and rough
On my throat, my pulse . . .

Someone passed, we stopped.
Then more, kiss me more, our
Faces hot in the snow . . .
My hands inside your coat,
Your black wool coat.
Your shirt,

White cotton, stiff,
Pulled it from your jeans
So I could—
Could reach the skin of
Your back, all, there, all
Fevered and smooth.

Another Time

One hoarse word,
I would have stayed.
Instead, his question
Hovered
Like a scent, cold
Scent of night snow,

Remembered,
A mockery of white
Petals at our feet.
(Which? Which?)
Truly
I loved them both.

They Cruised the Rappahannock Early in the Spring

I *knew* I should have pinned that gold ring to the sail.
    Because if you lose your jewelry when you go in for a swim,
    They give you a cheap speckled mirror, on a crooked nail.

Nana said that's not a very good hem, or hymn, or him.
    The Captain said keep your eye on her, she weaves.
    But I'm served only liquids: coffee, water, soda, gin:

How can a colorful scarf or throw rug be made from *these*?
    And it's strictly my job to pass out the geography books.
    And I'm constantly asked, "The direction, please."

"You mean of the river?" "No. The direction of hooks."
    "Well . . . It depends on how you hold it!" "Of course,
    Silly, how *do* you?" "Hmm. I don't *have* a hook. Took it

*Some*where . . . But I lost my wedding ring. And my horse,
    Too. Hal went and sold my horse Red Wing. Back in Ohio."
    "Which direction? Up? By the way, have you seen Lars?"

"I'm sorry. I don't know a Lars." "You don't know
    Lars Johnson? Well, I'll swan." "I know a *Cyn*thia Johnson."
    "Oh? Is Arlene Johnson your wife or your lover?" "No!

I mean neither. I'm a *woman*." "You say you're lonesome?"
    "Yes but that's not—" "Did you remember your Lithium?"
    "No but that's not—" "Is Arlene Johnson handsome?"

"No, I'd say pretty. She's a *woman*. Except it's Cynthia,
    Though. You keep saying Arl—" "WATCHIT!!" "That rail
    Doesn't always hold." "Oh, *look!* Japonica! Forsythia!"

Linear

When he looks at the others, I mean
When he not-looks at me,
That leaves me free
To memorize
The shirted shape for his back,
The sinuous lines throughout his hair,
Those, yes, and the rivery veins of his hands.

And when, on one of the nights,
It falls out that we walk back together,
It falls out that we descend into the formal garden,
It falls out that we take seats on respective ends of a bench,
I fall to measuring, think in shapes, in gradations:
Mountain, sky, their joinder in fog. Amazing,
The range of the night-grays.

We need a remark; I make it:
"Amazing, the range of grays at night.
Those shrubs look like granite, and the way they're spaced,
They make me think of tombstones."
"Yeah."
Mountain, sky . . .
"Yeah, it's strange." Joinder in fog . . .

The wine from the reception dizzies my faculties, his being here
Addles me, thrills me, to think, his heart
Beating under his shirt, my heart
Losing its grip, I
Glimpse—
I can't have seen that— bright return? not only against the rule
Against touch, untested, but against

A ban I already know
Intimately:
I'm not desirable.
I'm not prepared for desire.
If by night I feel a pull, by day I re-say, it's delusion.
Then who is this actress, surfacing?
Speechless,

For if,
For even one second,
I 'part my lips,' if I tip
Towards him, even one inch, that inch
Could collapse the meter between us—second into instant—then
The face
Will be

Yanked away.
"Are you enjoying it here?"
I blink, I swallow, "Oh, yes!"
Swallowed kiss ≠ swallowed word;
Swallowed word ≠ swallowed tear;
Swallowed tear ≠ swallowed kiss.
Any 2 or all 3 may ensue at once.

But coincidence ≠ cause-&-effect.
Things to keep separate, straight.
He: "Well, I'm—
Pretty tired, should probably be finding my room."
Kept separate, kept straight. He continues, "Are you . . . ?"
"Oh, I think I'll stay here
Awhile."

"Well," he stands,
He has stood, he is taking a stand,
He has stood, he is going, I remember some lines I have learned:
If the lady and gentleman wish to take their tea in the garden,
If the lady and gentleman wish to take their tea in the garden . . .
"Yes, good night."
This is how

I can prevent calling his name out after him: Memorize,
Memorize his gait, his trousers, memorize
The four garden steps, he climbs,
Still noting the steps,
He's left,
Again note the shrubs.
Memorize the trapezoid roof of that

Shed, the studied, faceted lid of the gazebo,
Vertical pines, horizontal pine-shadows, stripes across ground.
Sky, fog, their joinder. Law
Despite the mountains.
I shut my eyes,
And on and on, the night-singing insects, those makers of round,
Keep on, and on . . .

I press my mouth, into my palm, hard,
And on, they sound. One form
Merging from myriad
Participants,
Seeming to know
When to come in, and when
To leave off, knowing start without cost, stop without halt.

Unheroic Couplets

i.
I had thought my two palms
Measurers enough:

His worth, my love:
The counterweights.

ii.
I had thought we'd be held
As in

Palms of hands—
My flats of land, his dunes of sand,

My grasses, his waves,
Both moor-scapes, thereby more.

iii.
Symmetry, I thought:
Us: you and I; them: those two; that man, that woman;

Walkers, under field-sky, under sea-sky, free.
What shit.

iv.
What on earth made me think
My love, his worth, got weighed

In the first place, in the same scale. Here
Where the ceiling has mirrors, the walls . . .

Where the ceiling has mirrors, the walls . . .
The detailed gilt clock, little crystal lamps.

I'm like the cartoon hippo. "The Night of the Dance."
Stupid choice: ruffles.

v.
Here's the comparison
In this world: not

My love and his worth;
But my love for him and his

"Feelings" for me. What?
A kind of flat

Approbation? a slight
Asexual 'she's all right'?

vi.
Ludicrous. Nay. Grotesque!
The kisses I'd have given him,

Which of the multiple touches:
Ridiculous. My love, like my body, outsized:

Shameful reflection
Asserted in the selfsame mirror that holds

Him tête-à-tête with his princess:
She of pale taffeta, she of pale wine,

Lovely, if callow (but I'm not mean-spirited by
Nature, I'm not all hideous there).

vii.
That raises, however, the other
Comparison: herself and myself:

The acknowledgment-of-beauty gauge:
Moi: nil; elle: galore.

But I will not let
My monstrous shadow fall over him;

Him, the lover,
Whom I desire, who desires

Her, who bends to her, cupping
Each word of hers, fragile—

viii.
So I go outside, where my person can be swallowed.
I say to my vast love: starve.

Pentacle

TRUTH.
Undesired, undesirable, I yet desire

LIE.
Or did. Love, frustrated long enough,
Ceases to SPROUT VINES, like philoDENdron,
Stops boinking bo-kays like a goddamn CLOWN,
DeSISTS all the obSESSing on KISSes and NAMES

WISH.
And names and beCOMES: a cold   blue   sphere

POEM.
A three-inch sphere of cold blue steel
Polished to perfection and sent into space
To orbit, fast, fast, effortless, and fast;

ANALOG.
Its music   is John Adams's *HARMONIELEHRE.*

Chromatic Scales Against Impossible Loves

Sunday Dusk

Now work   now work   now work
    gives way   gives way
        to hue   to hue
            now hue   now hue
                to tones   to tones
                    of dark   of dark
                        now hearts   now hearts
                        now hearts   take on
                            take on   full weight
                            full weight   in in-
                                in in-   crements
                                  crements   like Bach
Now back   now back   now back   like Bach
    to work   to work
        now work   gives way
            to hue   now hue
                now hue   to tones
                    to tones   of dark
                    of dark   now, heart
                        now, heart   now hearts
                        take on   take on
                          full weight   full weight
                          in in- in in-   in in-
                                crements   like Bach
Like BACH like Bach like bach like bach like Bach like BACH

Boy Unobscured on the Highest Riser

Some clumsy hand spilled mimeograph ink
across this boy's face before he was even born. Now it clashes
with his orange blazer, which is, however, the same as the other boys. The
girls wear black satin dresses, their sleeves and skirts cut like petals. When
a boy on the front row sings a solo, the boy in the back row

Mouths the words. On the ride home in the
bus the color of goldenrod, the boy partnerless in the back
row sees lizards gigantic in the shape of distant hills, and in the clouds
behind the hawks, a school of dolphins—no, they are swordfish. Tonight,
an only child in his parents' farmhouse, he will practice his electric guitar
without plugging it into his amp. Then he will draw a man made entirely
of lightning, and a man made of leaves, and a man

Of ice. Past midnight, in bed, he
imagines himself on the wings of a dragon. They ride the
curve of the earth, follow the Andes as they snake, glide, over Antarctica,
and out, on past the moon, and the planets, and the stars. He taps each
one with his stick

Of pure crystal. He dreams he has red
lacquer balls and his sheets are white. Next, there is a kitchen
with yellow walls. A girl he knows concentrates at the table, playing a
board game of some kind or working a jigsaw puzzle, and the pieces are
bright. "Your hair is so beautiful," he says; her hair gleams black in the
sun, and he wants to touch it to his lips and his eyelids. She hands him a
sort of cord or whip with a button in the handle. "That's the panic
button," she says, "and whenever you want me to come back,

Just press it." A swimmer, not
necessarily himself, is circling the rim of a tank like an otter,
with a blanket over his head, pressing the button frantically. The dreamer
is in a boat with the girl then, and petals—they are bright—roses and
redbud—drift by from upriver. They come to a pier strung with lights.
Little white stars. A party. No choice but to go. Everyone's dancing, and
they're all good-looking, too, in shirts of red with green palm trees, and
yellow with maroon palm trees, and aqua with orange

Parrots. He has on his Grateful Dead
T-shirt. She has a rose tattoo on her left shoulder. Odd he'd
never noticed it before. "Go on and dance with one of these guys," he
either says or thinks he says. But she says, "You. I'd rather dance with
you." And he does, too, he dances, he stomps, his teeth pressed into his
lip. He jerks, awake,

Awake. The boy's initials, carved into
his silver maple headboard with his first pocketknife, emerge
into view from the dawn. In the pre-action safety of that light, he plans
his day's work: a cometlike figure: its face will be the paper left white, its
features will be drawn with only the lightest possible strokes of India ink,
as if laid down with an eyelash. The face itself, which is in right profile,
has eyelashes laid down that way. All the purple from the face has gone
into the comet's tail. This part will be done with oil pastels, in the
outlying art room at school, beside a dusty window. The purple is
stranded in with brown from his hair, and black from hers, and orange,
because he likes it, and because it is the color of all the boys' blazers. This
tail flares, half flame and half waterfall. The comet rushes to a place in
space, where shame doesn't puddle in the heart.

Girl at Sewing Machine

(After a painting by Edward Hopper)

It must be warm in the room, walls the color of oversteeped tea,
    the sun high,
Coating the yellow brick exterior of the apartment building,
    angling in on
The girl, stripped down to camisole and petticoat, sewing.
    She's a busty girl,
Soft, no doubt perspiring, slippery under her breasts, moisture
    trapped on the back of
Her neck, under all that chestnut hair. She doesn't notice it,
    though; you can see
She's intent on her seam. She doesn't slump over the machine
    but bends from the hip,
Her spine as attuned as her hands. Her feet, though not shown
    in the painting,
Are bound to be pudgy, are probably bare, pumping the treadle
    ka-chunk, ka-chunk, ka-chunk

But that's unconscious. Her point of concentration is the needle,
    silver, quick,
Its chick chick chick chick chick, necessity to keep the material
    in perfect position,
Position. What is she making? The fabric looks heavy and yet
    billowy, like
Whipped cream, or cumulus clouds; certain girls, while large, move
    with grace (when nobody's
There) but in public, conceal, or try to conceal, their bodies
    beneath long clothes.
They favor long hair, feeling it wimples and veils embarrassment.
    Yes, I know this girl.
Only in her room, only when unseen, can she relax at all, peel off
    a hot blouse,
A brown skirt, like the one heaped on her bed in the background,
    take pleasure in

A good hairbrush, the bottle of scent on the dresser, the picture
    of her own choosing

On the wall. Whatever she's making—let's go ahead and say it's
    a dress for herself—
She is not, as you might think, dreaming of a party, a dance,
    or a wedding. No, she's
Deciding to flat-fell that seam—time-consuming, but worth it—
    stronger, better-looking.
I'm sure she knows by now not to expect much attention from boys.
    She's what? twenty?
Eighteen? She will, in time, use many words to describe herself,
    not all of them bad;
But not once will one of them be "pretty," or "beautiful." Those
    aren't for a fat girl
Though she can take a mass of cloth, and a cast-iron machine,
    and make a lovely shape.

III.

The Shooting Party

(After a painting by J. J. Herring)

The all-red
Apples,
Grounded.

And the pink
Roses, whose nature
Is to wander, to discontain

The stonemason's jardiniere;
Whose fate is to fragment . . . petals all over the stairs . . .
Flagrant fragrance on the air . . . . .

And lupines—red, orange, red-orange—
Spiked in their god-given shapes—
Stiff flames, steep-angled torches ——

The man has just presented
The woman the bird, killed
Himself, the bullet fired

From his own gun; it took great skill.
The woman—sidesaddle on a fine trained bay standing still—
Permits the dead bird, lying, limp on her gloved right palm,

Her riding whip lax in her left hand's fingers. Tranquil,
Tranquil, her gaze fixed straight ahead at nothing the painter
Included, while the man peers at her face . . . peers, that is,

Up— at her face. His stance: planted: dust-ground:
His two booted legs and the butt of the gun: a brown tripod,
Like three saplings. (All don't survive: limited room.)

He holds the vertical gun by its barrel
The way a woman holds a broom
When she stands in the doorway, ever

Looking out . . . . .
In a parallel dumb show, the lad, maybe twelve,
Peers into the horse's face,

Proffers, in his upturned cap,
A gather of apples,
Apples the creature apparently

Feels no need for, indeed seems unaware of,
Though who knows what thought
Fills a horse's mind with what space?

The bird, being dead,
Has presumably emptied its eyes.
The only eyes

On the bird at the moment
Are those of the cat.
This cat, sleek-backed and curvy,

Alone, in this picture,
Inclines to
Motion: rampant, as though about to

Clamber up the horse's leg to its wither, to
The bird.
Had the cat itself killed the bird, as a cat

Will do—even tame cats will do—
In order to make of it a gift for its human,
No issue of blame

Would arise.
But as it is, I think,
The subject of this work remains

The man: the shooting party: the party who shoots.
His eyes, his gesture, the object he has given the woman
Seem somehow to constitute . . . . .

How could this be said?——
Some wordless, unsayable, unspeakable
Apologia:

I must
Pierce,
I must, and leave a red slit.

If you insist
On looking
As if you could fly,

It becomes my part
To stop you. Anything
To keep the sky mine, anything,

To keep you, here, on this earth,
KEEP you
WITH me, for I love you!

Understand
I am weak; I am cursed; I prefer
To marvel at the beautiful

Plummet.
Better to feel the awe I feel
When the killed one falls than have

To hear the free one crying always
"Look here! I'm alive!"
"And God," he continues,

"That *fiend*, whom *I* resemble, makes it seem *my* fault.
It is not my fault. It is not my fault.
Maybe it could be *your* fault. Would not that be *less* terrible?"

Not a very good
Painting, actually.
The individuals are rendered well, particularly

The animals, and plants.
But overall the proportions are off
So that: although

The horse is only slightly too small for the woman,
And the man only slightly too large for the woman,
The man ends up positively looming compared to the horse.

And the "rose-cheeked" lad
Is nearly
The size of the man, looks very much like him

In fact. Probably they both
Look like the painter
Did, when painting; did when young; or

Younger yet. The boy's face . . .
Longing, eloquent. And the woman . . . . . the woman
Wears a wide black skirt.

To a Woman with a Satchel

You sit, continent, in
An interior room in a large institution,
Law-books silent and door-slams
Echoing elsewhere . . .

Your heart, though, your heart
Sees
Your body apace on the hills
Fast heart and fast body and mind

Anything but numb, yet painless,
Free from
The presence that led you to
Grip your thumbs

I love you, I love you . . .
Unanswered.
Slamming echoing elsewhere.
All oceans are far, the hills, near.

Fast heart and fast body and then
Rest, within the tall grass.
Someday you and the grass
Will be truly alone together insensate.

(envoy)

But hear: the wind or some form
          of air, of existence, moves
Through all five with one message: *this
          is not evil, do not be ashamed
                    of this*

The Visited Stream

(Three poems after Aleksandr Pushkin)*

"FOUNTAIN AT TSARSKOYE SELO"

The woman has not dropped the urn and broken it on a rock.
Contentedly the woman sits, and holds the full urn.
As usual, the water does not dry up.
The woman sits, awhile, content, by the visited stream.

---

* From the marvelous source poems, I have kept the titles, but have reversed at least one term in each line, either by negation—e.g., instead of waited for, didn't wait for—or by substitution—e.g., instead of miraculously, as usual, instead of eternal, visited, instead of young, old, instead of old, young, etc.

"Young Mare"

Old stallion, disgrace!
But never mind.
I guess you're used to
Your tame spirit.

For you, unlike for me,
Time is running out.
Why not here?
In the narrow slanted field.

Decline to lift your feet,
The air so heavy. Accept
This closing,
Rheumy eyes.

Go ahead. I won't delay
Your sinking down
To your failed knees
With my lovable voice.

"TO MY NANNY"

Faithless deserter from an unhappy time,
Enemy! my vital young nanny—
'With someone' in the deep pine-forest.
You didn't expect, didn't wait for— me!

Your window upstairs left blank of you—
A lack in the place of the guardian.
The knitting needles you were supplied
Cast aside by your smooth nimble hands.

You glance at the just-used gate,
At the dazzling, immediate road.
Satiation, hope— they, Rejoicer, lighten
Your heart, long ago. Now you know.

Four Fountains

four fountains which refreshed his youth
to shoot out shining in their shaped ways
A RIDDLE IN THE EXETER BOOK

I.
Plank, once painted, now
Silvery.
        Sail, still implied,
Waning waterwise.

II.
Warm yourself. Wish with
The solstice,
        drown with her. Jon-
Gleur, go down the dark.

III.
Your face with its fresh
Day's beard felt
        slightly sandy
To me. & so warm.

IV.
Things with all their surge.
S. S's.
        Blue horses. The
Hands-on hallowing.

IV.

Girls' Names

```
[Aunt Consuelo's voice.^you are an ELIZABETH.^|WHICH|
[M[Now at five as I turn up the wick by the window]M]
[A[I see the lights moving at Sarah and Mary's. By]A]
[R[ §Susan Stewart of Philadelphia, Pen. in her §  ]R]
[I[poem  §   §   §   §   §   §   §  "The]Y]
[A[א Factory Girls Get Up to Read Shakespeare"  Ψ]?]
[N[πJ§u§l§i§e§t§    §L§a§v§i§n§i§a§    §C§o§r§d§e§l§i§a¥]A]
[N[S W A N N A N O A   N O R T H   C A R O L I N A]U]
[E[~~Dear Rebecca,       ~Ω~         Jan. 9, '90~~]N]
[B[      Francine:navy blue   sweater,  rose  stripe.       ]T]
[O[~  Lucy:black Angora  sweater,  sky blue  beads.    ~]M]
[R[    Lee:blue denim shirt,  rich  burgundy   scarf.     ]A]
[U[~Eleanor  W:burgundy/olive   intricately   knit.     ~]R]
[C[      Ann S:black sweater,  skirt,  tights,  boots.      ]Y]
[H[~    Mary:I was there but what was I saying?      ~]?]
[S[    Probably  the  black calico  Skirt  that  Sara      ]T]
[G[~  gave me, or else "Old Blue"; brown  shoes   ~]A]
[R[      black  tights,  and  either  my  Olive  tunic  or  ]L]
[A[~∞~  my gray turtle, both of whom love me.  ~∞~]L]
[N[E l l e n s   f i n e   W e   w i s h   y o u &]M]
[D[ j  '  '  '  '  '  '  '  '  '  '  f ]A]
[M[ a    xxx    Hello Juliana?        xxx      o ]R]
[A[ p    Î    Hello Augusta?        Î      r ]Y]
[S[ o        What are you doing tomorrow?     s ]S]
[B[ n xxx      Sleeping,        xxx     y ]T]
[R[ i  Î          sleeping.        I [ t ]E]
[O[ c  *   *   *   *   *   *   *   *   h ]A]
[W[ a   **    **    **    **    **    **    ia ]R]
[N[By  Eleanor  Ross  Taylor  in  her  poem  "New  Girls."]N]
[C[      E.R.T.    b.Norwood  N.C.  Lives  in  Charlotte's-]S]
[H[ville, V i r g i n i a; also Ten. & Florida.      ]I]
[E[H e a t h e r   h a d   b e e n   w i t h   u s]K]
[C[ + ? + ¿ + ? + ¿ + ? + ¿ + ? + ¿ + ? + ¿ + ? + ]N]
[K+]    The whippoorwill is surer of her name     [?E]
[D++]    than we are sure of anything.       [??W]
[R+++]By- - - - - K a t h a r i n e - - - - -Jo[????]
[E++++]Haddox Privett of Pawnee Oklahoma in [Eliz]
[S+++++] her poem "Watching My Daughter Sew" [Bishop]
[S]H U G  A N N  & M A R I A  4  M E   L O V E  ML[X]
```

To a Girl with a Satchel

Soon you will have a car and then, you will know
Where to go—
                    Eastward, Scrub Oak Kingdom
              the busiest squirrels, the bossiest blackbirds

And West   to the fields   to the everything-stretching
Ground in furrows   crops in rows
     dirt road   bar ditches   sunflowers   barbwire
Where meadowlarks sing sharp yellow song
And doves   in gray   say   day here   day over

                                        South
Through the Arbuckle Mountains
                    the timetable
                         tilts and layers
                    all the different striations
              it used to be under the sea

To the North and the East, you're about to discover
What they call the Osage
                    all rolling hills but flatter—
                         like plains only
                              more rolling than that—

                                             horizon-to-

Horizon—grass—you
Will write Grass, like Ocean,
Because it's Full of Sound moving all around
And there

Will see the red-tailed hawk, will watch him soar
And when, in empty air, you hear his high high cry

                                        your heart!
                                        your mate!

Will feel a body could die
Here is my wish— May someone know

To bury you there when you do really die
Or scatter your ashes

Which will it be? Which will you need
                              more—
A moment flying in wind
                    or an eon laid down with rain

Rife Sill

I come to a window with yellow curtains, picture
Observing an abstract number of green tomatoes,
A cake of bow rosin, amber scarred over with white.
I tell you, I fell in love with a boy, not because

He played the cello, but because I could imagine him
Playing the cello. From a dream I picked his door,
Turquoise paint, not new. He sent me a postcard
From Budapest, that much remains true. He was Jewish.

In history, one walks where two walked before, alongside
The Danube, in my mind, curtains splay in a gust,
Sheet music takes wing, in his life, he turned up his collar.

Beyond the blue-green door, lovers laugh, oh they are
Jars of honey. A splash of sapphire emotes
Inside one of them, cast by a cobalt, diagonal pane.

24 Doors

for Joel Bettridge

Thank you for the broom for whisking the sins off my shoulders
Before I go in the first door.

Thank you for the flight of steps that allows me to stall before I
Have to consider the second door's white arch and go in.

Thank you for the row of pineapples ripening, distracting me from
How low and narrow and unattractive the third door seems that I
Must go in.

Thank you for the latch that keeps other people from noticing me
Once I have gone in the fourth door.

Thank you for the candles in their chandeliers, and later in their
Sconces, to cheer me as I go in the fifth, sixth, & seventh doors.

Thank you for the entryway pile of wooden benches whose jumbled
Impermanence makes me feel better about the stoniness of the
Eighth door I must go in.

Thank you for the diving board featured near the ninth door just
In case I want to get it over quickly, this matter of going in.

Thank you for the letters of the sign that reminds me I am not the
First to go in the tenth door.

Thank you for the rottenness of the cloth that mottles my sight as
I try to be unafraid of going in the eleventh door.

Thank you for the example of the swirls and liquid commas that
Decorate the tilted square, the twelfth door I go in.

Thank you for the wheels, their plangent turning beneath me, blind
Inside the yellow cart that carries me, going in the thirteenth
Door.

Thank you for the semicircles and the half-moon that grant me
Yellow, red, and white designs to wear as I go in the fourteenth
Door.

Thank you for the eye of the spiral that gives me the illusion
That the fifteenth door is nothing but a target for going in.

Thank you for letting me glimpse the sunlight burnishing the red
Sandstone frame of the sixteenth door, the poet's door where,
Though I didn't, I could have gone in.

Thank you for the tapestry that spares me direct contact with the
Groundwater infiltrating the tunnel walls I brush up against,
Having gone in the seventeenth door.

Thank you for the light light, and for the dark dark, for the
Flattened granite shore boulders, and for the blue streaks like
Ocean waves, and for the nearly transparent sky that illumines the
View beyond door eighteen, where I can look without having to go
In if I don't want to.

Thank you for the iron ring on the inside casket lid, although I
Do know it can only be pulled, not pushed, when it's time to go
In door nineteen.

Thank you for the three priests who have already been inside the
Twentieth door and come back out again, who have expected me
Kindly, who have cleared a space on the floor before me, before I
Go in.

Thank you for the little child sent to dig my grave beside a boat
In the mud, after I have gone, sent in the newness of the twenty-
First door.

Thank you for the reeds that, centuries later, will bend and
Cross, and their shadows bend & cross, reflected in the water
That's collected to cover the hole that I went in when it was my
Twenty-second door.

Thank you for the mast for the black sail, the moon on that mast,
The hunchbacked going in, to the sounds of the twenty-third psalm.

God, heartbeat of heartbeats, let me come in.

Both

1. *For Mary Walsh Webb Haddox*

When

Body inhales, soul

Extends freezing palms; when body

Exhales, soul folds palms on chest. End this

Servant's life on an inhale: gesture

Of grace, not

Rest.

1898 – 1988

2. *A Mary (1948–   )*

This is like the
Black gondola! sliding
Sliding in to sleep . . . But if I fall
Asleep, will I fall off the divan? Wallpaper at
Granny's=blackboard at school=where
The light can take its nap.
It's mowing
Outside, mowing
On Sunday. Thunder, way
Far away. Tip— me-o-ver-pour-me-
Out. This book's my favorite, you can hold it
To sleep going. These horses—
They're my favorite. *Red*
Horses. Franz
Marc. I like
Him—with his foot up—he's
My favorite. Might color a new girl—
Like the *sea green* girl with *forest green* eyes
Just like her but *cadet blue* with *corn-*
Flower blue eyes and long
Apricot braids

Lulling

These are the words — the first verse of Robert Burns's "Flow Gently, Sweet Afton" — of the song my mother would sing me:

Flow gently, sweet Afton, among thy green braes!
Flow gently, I'll sing thee a song in thy praise!
My Mary's asleep by thy murmuring stream—
Flow gently, sweet Afton, disturb not her dream!

I remember especially hearing it when I was around five, on the front porch in the summer . . . where we could "catch the breeze."

This is the tune:

My Son Ted

Mrs. McGrath lived near the seashore
For the space of seven long years or more,
When she spied a ship comin' into the bay
'Tis my son Ted, would ya clear the way?'
IRISH SONG

Weather was lake and I took you to see it,
Your mittened hand diminutive in mine . . .
You are as tall, now, as some trees, the new-planted.
You take the steps two at a time.
The leather straps on your man's wrists
Darken with sweat when you drum. You drum
Like a form of attack,
You drum with a vigor resembling your birth.
Weather did not have a watch.
Weather was blue chipped paint on cement steps.
Weather was red of our geraniums,
Nectarine-fuzz texture, geranium leaves,
Pungency, geranium redolence.
Weather was warmth of sun on a pine porch floor.
Weather was cool cement of the steps, sitting on them.
Weather was for your clothes,
Shorts and no shirt, a little boy's chest,
Jeans and a T-shirt, and a flannel shirt,
And a corduroy coat, with a hood, and wool mittens.
After years, after thousands of miles, I fill
The bathtub that only I use.
The adolescent boy's yellow oxford-cloth shirt, un-tucked-in.
Ruddy hand offering acorns
To the doe by the swing set.
The smoke and the sandstone one smell.
Not really cold yet, but still,
A fire in the fireplace, a way to say Fall,
And extra wood beside it.
In the closet, extra blankets laid in.
Lamp inside, on.
On the porch, I lingered,

Took in the last of that dusk, the damp
In that air, the cool in that air,
Before going in to start supper.
Inside the doorway, the switch for the porch light,
The yellow-bulbed porch light,
For when he would be coming in, just a minute . . .
Maybe he could come to visit me here,
Maybe he could come on the plane? . . .
The quilt-top someone never got around to quilting
Covered the window, I liked it that way, the sunlight
Coming in through small shredded places
Made positive chinks and the child was safe in those days,
His hair, in coppery ringlets,
His fingernails, and toenails, soft from the bath . . .
The clippers made not-a-loud click.

Her Door

for my daughter Sara Marie

There was a time her door was never closed.
Her music box played "Für Elise" in plinks.
Her crib new-bought— I drew her sleeping there.

The little drawing sits beside my chair.
These days, she ornaments her hands with rings.
She's seventeen. Her door is one I knock.

There was a time I daily brushed her hair
By window light— I bathed her, in the sink
In sunny water, in the kitchen, there.

I've bought her several thousand things to wear,
And now this boy buys her silver rings.
He goes inside her room and shuts the door.

Those days, to rock her was a form of prayer.
She'd gaze at me, and blink, and I would sing
Of bees and horses, in the pasture, there.

The drawing sits as still as nap-time air—
Her curled-up hand— that precious line, her cheek . . .
Next year her door will stand, again, ajar
But she herself will not be living there.

Oklahoma Passover

A slam in the loft   mouse-scuttle up-attic   a rock of the rocker
    the uniform shudders   hail spits in the yard   sky gone from
      normal to black   no time   the parlor storm-dark

The rose in the bible   the pictures   forgotten the hall
    storm-dark and no time   the bedroom   the old woman gaping
      she'll have to be carried   the parlor   the porch

Wind shredding the cottonwood   weather vane squawking
    the chickens all squawking   all pecking the hailstones
      the old mother squawking   Oh Honey Oh Honey

Wind whipping her bandages   spilling her toes   the air
    gone from dark to green   and the mare   the mare
      the mare fast-galloping   west-a   west-a   west

      The cellar door bangs
        and down, go
          down.

      The twister veers off
        to the north/northeast.
          The tailwind, her son,

      Looks around,
        shrugs his shoulders,
          moves on.

      The weather vane's
        N
          —that's all they took.

      An omen: Not us.
        Not us.
          Amen.

The Sign of the Cohens Carved on a Gravestone

November 9, 1938, Stillwater, Oklahoma

"May Brandenburg called today."

"Hm," (chewing).

"She wanted to know if she could borrow the Waterford punch bowl."

"No." Then. To me. "Salt and pepper, darling."

Mama presses. "It's for her daughter's wedding.
You know her daughter's marrying that McCollum boy."

Papa fends. "This is of interest to me? Since when
Are we invited to their weddings, I'd like to know."

"Well, she didn't inv—"

"Of course not."

"I don't think that's anything to do with it, Sam.
We barely know them."

"Yeah, well let's keep it that way." Then to Harriet
He says, "What're-ya? digging for gold in them thar peas?
Just eat already."

Mama says. "One bite, sweetheart."
She says to Papa, "I think this is something we should both
Discuss."

"What's to discuss? The answer is no."
To me, "Enid, how many times to I have to remind you? Do not
Swing your feet at the table. Please."
To Mama, "So how does she come to have knowledge of this swell
Punch bowl in the first place, I'd like to know."

Mama tilts her head, "Oh, she dropped by the other day,
Her and Ruby Upshaw, collecting for the Red Cross, you know,
The flood relief. So— it was a chilly day— I asked them in—
We had a little Lipton's tea— a few cookies— is this all right
With you, Mr. In-Charge-of-the-Household?"

"Great! Tea? Cookies? Charming!
Sure, why not, visit all you want. Believe me, I get plenty of
Their visiting down at the store." Then in a high squeaky voice,
"Oh, foot, Mr. Coe-hin. I jist cain't decide.
Rilly, I'm afraid that beige dudn do a thang for me (Mama's
Smiling) I sure do wish you had that in a yella.
I doan know— Ruby, what do you thank?"

So Mama's smiling, shaking her head. "Sam, Sam, will you
Listen to me? (Mama has one palm out)
I told her she could use it already."

Papa drops his knife and fork on his plate (big clatter)
Has both palms out, like to test for rain, looking at the ceiling,
Saying "By the Rivers of Babylon!"

Mama also has her shoulders up and both palms out
But together, like to single out a food on a holiday table,
"C'mon— a daughter's wedding— after all—"

Papa with his eyes closed is shaking his head saying "oy." Still
Shaking his head, eyes half open, a shrug, "oh well."

"A daughter's wedding—"

"Yeah, yeah, yeah." He holds up his pointer-finger. "As long
As they don't break it!"

"I'm sure they'll be very careful . . ." Mama . . .

And Papa . . .

Look at the punch bowl, on its doily, on the sideboard . . .

*

It looked so crystally,
There, in the low west sun,
Holding oddments visible through glass, seen
As fractured by the facets, into chips of color,
But known in experience, whole. A button, some coins,
A spool of thread, a German stamp on its envelope corner,
A couple of Parcheesi men.

Photographs (for our children)

(After a film by Edit Koszegi, Sandor Simo, & Andras Suranyi)

. . . like a child. Said "Look at the finch in that tree!"
Like a child. Wouldn't speak one word of the War,
Said "Look at the lizard, how fast he is, see?"

. . . came back a hag! How could I love her? Slowly
Things worked out. But never the same as before,
And her barren. "Look at the finch in that tree!"

. . . they rounded us up, my son screaming 'Let me
Through!'—he was so in love—'I think I saw her!'
"Look at . . ." 'Le-ah!!' ". . . lizard, how fast he is, see?"

. . . the whole time I had to sleep with enemy
Soldiers, I thought about my little daughter . . .
Look away, doll, "Look at the finch in that tree!"

. . . stick-limbed, lousy, blind. She whispered 'It won't be
Long.' Eighty-two! Kept dropping that chocolate bar.
Blind. "Look at the lizard, how fast he is, see?"

. . . crossed to the civilian train. My old Da', he
Wouldn't come with. I— covered the yellow star.
(Da' don't shout out, "Look at the finch in that tree!")
I— "Look at the lizard, how fast he is, see?"

Proverbs (for the confectioner's apprentice)

Only to a florist with a pencil are circles roses.

Fresh egg, fragile egg.

After sculpting, leaves have names; during it, not even you do.

The warmer the wish, the redder the star.

A jealous heart is like ants in the sugar.

Toss it, fix it, frost it.

Poem to Gregory Orr

With the others, we assembled,
Two, half in love with our many disagreements, half alike,

As curlicues and zigzags
Never hooked, sometimes brushed, we,

With the others, assembled.
Always it was intricate

                         like
Classical Indian music, *raga*, certain notes

                                  set
To take place, in order arranged,

                                        but
In the gaps, anything could happen
Curlicues in space, in time, zigzags,

                                              or
The other way around,
                      particles

Free-floating, caught, lasting
For hours, all night, ten days

Forming, and dissolving, and reforming
And sometimes the most intricate figure becomes the ground,

Then a startling new figure breaks through.
The people had sparklers, and were tracing big circles

And writing little squiggles, too, and little names.
But you— you felt a line of Whitman's shoot

And as it passed, loud, through your body
You got free—

You threw your whole sparkler high in the air—
Across a momentary dark, a delible

                                                arc—
You will be remembered for it,

At least as long as I
Live. You will be remembered for the way, reading poems,

You would set down the sounds, with such
                                                care,

Not only with your voice but with your left hand, your maker's
Hand— word

Suspended between thumb and fingers, repeated, rhythmically,
Your gesture uniting *Ready* & *Now.*

At the dance the tenth night,
The same night you cast your sparkler to the heavens

With the others, we danced.
Always it was intricate. Dancing with you,

I was glad for my skirt, because it was allowed
                                                to twirl.

On the tenth afternoon, during my reading,
You mattered to me—

I will remember you
Sitting near the front of the amphitheater,

Your elbows on armrests, your fingers clasped loosely,
Your head down to listen, your eyes up to see.

And afterwards, you were the first to approach
To embrace me, to congratulate me—

But somehow, your face became another
                                                face

And other faces became other faces, I didn't discern
The spaces that must have occurred

                                        in among them,
I was going on— hello, hello, oh thank you—

                  *

Where did you go? Why didn't I keep you in view?

I didn't disintegrate. I only migrated a layer. We live
As in an electron microscope.

And die so?—your brother, out hunting, out of your sight, getting
Shot by you, somehow—do you think he may've migrated a layer?

I only know he bled.

Among Things Held at Arm's Length

They planted cedars around the farmhouses in those days:
Homeplace. Cedars are fast growers, and they mass, they're thick:
Windbreak. So when a thunderstorm would rant and rave and spew,
The cedars would take it, would wrestle the thing, stop it

At the windows. The people would be lying there a yard away
In nice dry bedclothes. The dog's eyes would be open, waiting.
And in the afternoon, which is the calm, why then the cedars

Would shift a little in the breeze, and their shadows
Would move all dappley on the windows, on the white windowsills.
This is a permanent thing, seen from cradles, seen from deathbeds.

*

A woman, for example, one of whose names was Muriel, had
Her window, her branch, her bird, her hour for the watch. Free,
Because she'd draped the dish towel over the dishes to dry; free,
Because she had a cocker spaniel pup on her lap, his head silky

To stroke; free, because by then she had mostly quit talking.
That a name means matters. What the name *is* doesn't, or, varies.
Pawnee County, Oklahoma. Place shows the difference between

Anywhere, which it can be, and *arbitrary*, which it can't. A time
All people find, a joint time, a time certain, not known,
Ordinarily, in advance. A time came and a Muriel died.

*

And when she was a bride, and even a young wife, her red-haired
Husband would come in from the field his energy scarcely
Diminished and he would pick her up around the waist and whirl
Her around in the dusty yard until her stockings would cowl

The tops of her laced-up shoes. She would laugh and he would
Smile. The first child was a daughter and they named her Armand,
A girl more somber than either parent, a girl with auburn hair;

Then a boy with clay red hair, Bryce, soon nicknamed "Brick";
Then a boy with hair the color of a new penny, Joe; then Rex,
With hair the color of an old penny; finally, a dark-haired girl,

*

Hair dark as Muriel's own, a joyous child, called Claudie Ann.
And the sodbuster's name, not to be omitted, was Arnold,
Which only Muriel ever voiced. To everyone else he was "Red."
His brother, whose real name even I don't know, was "Blue,"

On account of his coal black hair. The time came and the time
Came and the time came; the time will come and come and come
And come, for the littlest daughter, will come likewise.

With luck: a cedar branch, a wind, with luck a cardinal bird.
Hazel eyes, or blue or brown, or gray or green, the same for one
Whole lifetime. The pre-sunrise light is daily. Today

*

I just happened to see it. I aligned my palm with the horizon.

Poem

Then comes the pale figure:
                        animated inchling of light,
Running, not swift but steady,
                        running in a screen
Of hills, not hills but
                    undulations, gently torn
Strips in a tissue collage:
                    ten shades of green,
And four of yellow,
                and skyblue and aquamarine.
Thus you entitle your midsummer poem:
Pale Figure Running in Bright-Colored Landscape

MARY LEADER practiced law for many years in her home state of Oklahoma, first as Assistant State Attorney General and later as Referee for the Supreme Court of Oklahoma. While working as a lawyer, she earned a Master of Fine Arts from the Program for Writers at Warren Wilson College. Currently, she is the Creative Writing Fellow for Poetry at Emory University, where she also lectures in Literature and Law. Meanwhile, she is completing a doctorate in English and American Literature at Brandeis University.

This book was designed by Will Powers. It is set in Adobe Caslon type by Stanton Publication Services, Inc., and manufactured by BookCrafters on acid-free paper.